Richard Rogers

Richard Rogers

LOFT

Editor: Robert Torday / Richard Rogers Partnership

Editorial co-ordination : Aurora Cuito

Translation: Ana Peco/Lingo Sense

Copy-editing: Cristina Doncel

Graphic design: Philip Dennis / Emma Termes Parera

Editor's note: Thanks are due to both Lennart Grut and Jan Güell, colleagues at RRP who have supported and contributed to this book. I would also like to thank Philip Dennis at RRP whose skills as a graphic designer have been invaluable.

Photographers pages 6-7: Law Courts Antwerp, Katsuhisa Kida.
National Assembly for Wales, Andrew Holt.
New Area Terminal Barajas Airport, Amparo Garrido.
Las Arenas Barcelona, Eamonn O'Mahony.

ISBN: 84-95832-51-8
D.L.: B-46368-05

Editorial project

© LOFT Publications
Via Laietana 32, 4ffl Of. 92
08003 Barcelona. Spain
Tel.: +34 932 688 088
Fax: +34 932 687 073
loft@loftpublications.com
www.loftpublications.com

Printed by

Anman Gràfiques del Vallès, Spain

Over some three decades the Richard Rogers Partnership has attracted critical acclaim and dozens of prestigious international awards and honours. This book looks at the extraordinary range of work generated by the practice, from the celebrated schemes of the '70s and '80s such as the Centre Pompidou and the iconic Lloyd's of London building, right up to key projects as diverse as the Millennium Dome in London and a small school near Kyoto, Japan. All sixteen schemes, however disparate in terms of function, demonstrate themes which are central to RRP's design philosophy – flexibility, legibility and environmental responsibility – above all an emphasis on the importance of delivering sustainable buildings that celebrate people and public space.

RRP continues to engage in a broad range of projects. The practice is currently working on Barajas Airport, Madrid, Heathrow Airport's Terminal 5, the Antwerp Law Courts, a new National Assembly for Wales in Cardiff and the transformation of Las Arenas, a historic bullring in Barcelona, into a dynamic cultural and entertainment complex. Other schemes under way include a new cancer care centre in London, commercial office developments at Canary Wharf, London, a new library for the City of Birmingham, a 48-storey office tower at 122

Leadenhall Street in the City of London and a major mixed-use development in Korea.

Richard Rogers is Chief Advisor on Architecture and Urban Design to the Greater London Authority, and a member of the Mayor of Barcelona's Urban Strategies Advisory Council; he was also chairman of the British Government's Urban Task Force. This passion for urban design is reflected in much of the practice's ongoing masterplanning work – with significant projects currently under way in London, Lisbon and Rome and New York.

How will the Richard Rogers Partnership fare in the 21st century? The practice faces the future with a remarkably sure-footed team, building on the innovation and intelligence that continues to characterise an ever-expanding portfolio of work all over the world. From a winery near Valladolid to an acclaimed City Academy in one of London's most impoverished inner-city boroughs, the Richard Rogers Partnership demonstrates time and again an innate ability to respond imaginatively to the requirements of a specific project, always pushing technological boundaries in order to achieve the optimum solution.

Rogers House

This house, built for Rogers' parents, developed the vocabulary of Reliance Controls and of a slightly earlier house in Essex designed for Humphrey Spender. Now working independently of Team 4, Rogers again recalled the Case Study houses he had seen in California, especially the work of Raphael Soriano, and created a radical living space.

The scheme consists of two, simple single-storey pavilions carefully arranged within a deep garden plot opposite Wimbledon Common. The idea was that the house would be assembled rather than built – the framework consists of eight steel portals, three for the studio and five for the main house, with two portals removed to create a central garden courtyard. The idea was that this area could be in-filled should the needs of the owners change. The internal divisions and utilities were designed for maximum adaptability – the side walls are of plastic-coated aluminium panels joined with a neoprene zip system used on the Zip-Up house (the original technology was developed in the USA for refrigerated trucks). Similarly, the windows were off-the-shelf items used in contemporary bus design: sourcing components in this way optimised on both energy and mass-manufacturing quality.

Rogers sees a house as an exercise in overall design. It must incorporate the possibility of growth and change but be self-sufficient in itself. The Wimbledon house is, at the same time, ruthless in its straightforwardness and uncompromising use of mass-produced materials and beguiling in the elegance of its spaces, its carefully considered detailing, manipulation of scale and the relationship between the interior and exterior.

For Rogers, designing houses has been an important catalyst in the development of his architecture. In the hands of other modern architects, a house can be a perfect object. Rogers has never separated the design of individual houses from his concern for housing more generally. A private house, whether large and costly or small and economical, is a component in a new social architecture.

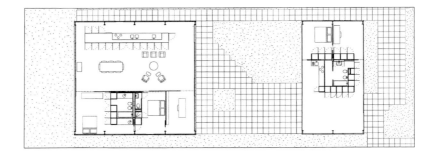

Centre Georges Pompidou

Designed in partnership with Renzo Piano, the Centre Pompidou was the building which brought Richard Rogers international fame. The scheme (won in competition) brought together the themes – skin and structure, technology and flexibility, movement and anti-monumentalism – which have characterised Rogers' architecture from the mid 1960s.

The architects envisaged their building as a cross between 'an information-oriented computerised Times Square and the British Museum', a democratic place for all people, all ages and all creeds, simultaneously instant and solemn, and the centrepiece of a regenerated quarter of the city. It was to be 'a giant climbing frame', the antithesis of existing cultural monuments. The completed Centre fully realises their intentions, miraculously fusing the spirit of 1968 with the ostensible aim of commemorating a conservative head of state.

Since half of the total available site was set aside by Rogers and Piano as a public square, the Centre had to be tall to accommodate the 90,000 square metres (one million square feet) of space demanded by the brief. The decision to place structure and services on the outside was driven primarily by the need for internal flexibility – the scheme provided huge expanses of uninterrupted space on massive, open floors nearly 50 metres deep. The staggering scale of these internal spaces took to extremes Rogers' concern to create space free from the intrusion of services and stairs (reflecting the influence of Kahn's doctrine of 'served and servant spaces') and these areas have proved to be highly adaptable, their character and use changing freely within the life of the Centre – there is no obvious hierarchy which separates art and learning from more mundane activities.

The structural system provided for a braced and exposed steel superstructure with reinforced concrete floors, realised with the help of the brilliant engineer Peter Rice. External services give scale and detail to the facades, while celebration of movement and access is provided by lifts and escalators which, like the services, were outside the covering of the building. The result is a highly expressive, strongly articulated building which came to be seen as a landmark in the development of High Tech (a term Rogers loathes).

Yet the achievement of Rogers and Piano at Beaubourg was broadly urbanistic as much as architectural. The building and great public square were intended to revitalise an area of Paris that had been in decline. The neighbouring Marais district, now vibrant and multi-cultural, underlines the enormous success of the Pompidou's role as a catalyst for urban regeneration, changing the character of Paris and laying the foundations for the later Grands Projets. It is as a place for people and a restatement of the fundamental Rogers belief that cities adapt to the needs of people (not vice versa) that the Centre must be counted one of the most significant post-war European buildings.

The Pompidou's radicalism is still striking and has proved attractive to a vast public: more than seven million people visit the building every year. The recent renovation prior to re-opening in 2000 significantly compromised the original design. Escalators have been installed from the foyer to the library, permanent exhibition spaces have been introduced and the public is now charged to use the escalators rising up the facade. That said, the building and its extraordinary contents remain as popular as ever, while crowds fill the square, clustering around musicians, acrobats and fire-eaters. Beaubourg – inside and out – remains as magnetic as ever.

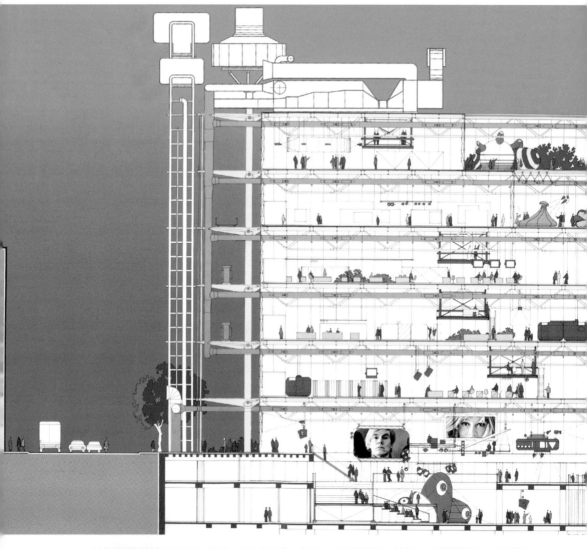

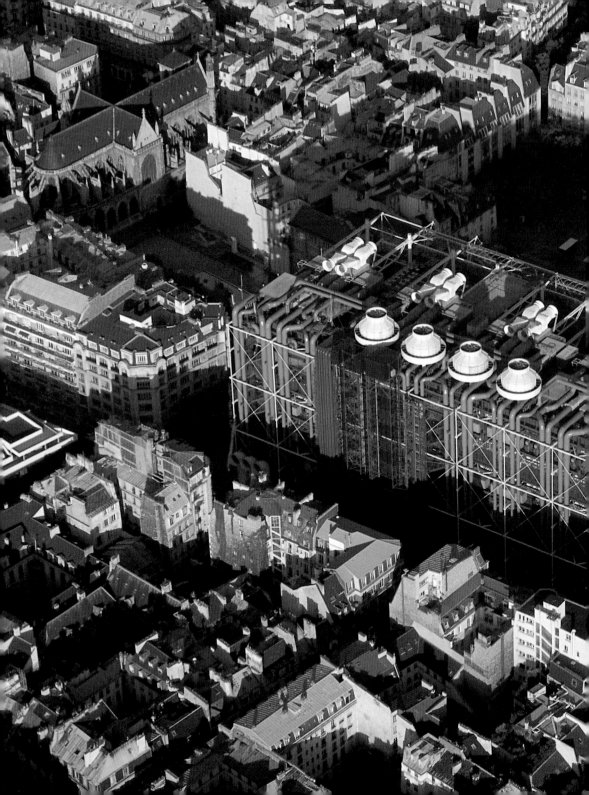

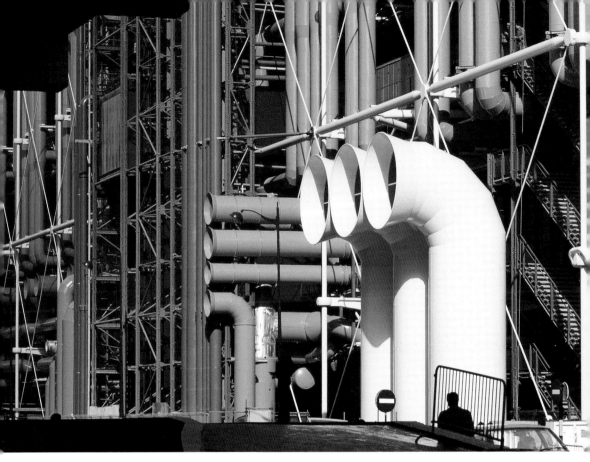

Lloyd's of London

Lloyd's of London is the world's greatest insurance market – a true market where insurance, rather than tangible goods, is traded. The competition for a new Lloyd's was won on the basis not of an architectural proposal but of a convincing strategy for the future of this key City institution. Lloyd's had moved the 'Room' – the centre of dealing operations – twice in 50 years and wanted a building which would provide for its needs well into the next century. It was also imperative that the members of Lloyd's could continue their operations unhindered during the rebuilding operation, which almost inevitably, involved the demolition and replacement of the existing 1928 building.

RRP proposed a building where the Room could expand (or contract), according to the needs of the market, by means of a series of galleries around a central space, with escalators and lifts providing easy access between floors. To maximise the usable space in the building, the practice banished the services to the perimeter. Servicing includes a high degree of air- conditioning reflecting the large population, intensive use of computers and the need to exclude noise.

Initially, it was proposed to construct Lloyd's, like the Centre Pompidou, in a steel frame but fire safety requirements made this impossible and concrete was used. The building was extensively clad in stainless steel. As the architectural form of the building evolved, particular attention was paid to its impact on the surrounding area and especially on the listed 19th-century Leadenhall Market, a structure which Rogers held in high regard. Instead of the great rectangle of Pompidou, Lloyd's became a complex grouping of towers, almost Gothic in feeling – an effect further enhanced when the upgrading of services meant the growth of the plant-room towers.

Lloyd's brought together the inspirations which had underlain RRP's architecture from the beginning. The plan was derived from Frank Lloyd Wright's Larkin Building, via Louis Kahn, while the look of the building was Futurist. The internal atrium, staggering in its scale and verticality, owed something to Paxton's Crystal Palace, a lost monument Rogers had venerated as one of the first modern buildings. The use of opaque glass, producing a subdued light, harked back to Pierre Chareau' s Maison de Verre in Paris, which Rogers had discovered while a student. The accretive, ad hoc quality of the building was obviously prefigured in Pompidou but is even more determined and uncompromising at Lloyd's – what had been a visionary dream in the 1960s had come to reality, and at the heart of the supposedly reactionary City of London. A failure of nerve on the part of Lloyd's management led to some compromises in the internal fit-out – the Lloyd's chairman now presides from a pseudo-Georgian office – but the 'boxes' where the insurance business is conducted are a happy reworking of the traditional arrangement. A further compromise reduced the degree of public space in the project – public lobbies of the Manhattan sort are alien to British traditions.

Lloyd's is one of the great architectural achievements of the 1980s, one of the buildings which confirmed Rogers' position in the front rank of British (and indeed international) architects. By the time of its completion, Post Modernism and Classicism were growing influences on the architectural scene in Britain and radical designs were suppressed, not least in the City. Yet Lloyd's has weathered a long period of design and construction to emerge as one of the greatest modern British buildings, one which balances technical efficiency with architectural expressiveness to produce an effect which must be called highly romantic and judged a very positive addition to the London skyline. Lloyd's has recast the image of modern architecture in Britain.

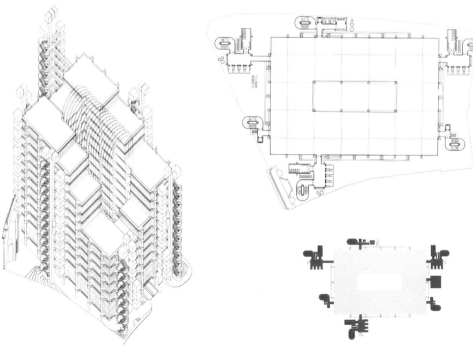

Inmos Microprocessor Factory

While Fleetguard had been designed with the needs of a sensitive site in mind, the INMOS scheme was seen as a model factory, suitable for construction in a wide variety of locations. The technical brief was demanding. Highly controlled conditions were required for the production of electronic microchips, with more conventionally serviced space housing offices, staff canteen and other facilities under the same roof.

The building had to be designed for fast construction (ready for operation within one year of starting on site) – which implied a high degree of off-site fabrication – and great flexibility. The context of the commission was a government-backed drive to expand the British microchip industry: the need was for specialised production space, to be available at the earliest possible opportunity.

RRP responded by producing a scheme which not only met the brief fully but was architecturally striking. The resulting building has great external presence and a strong sense of identity inside for those who work there.

The scheme is divided into 'clean' areas (that is, for microchip production) and 'dirty' (normally serviced ancillary) areas along a central promenade (or 'street') of more than 100 metres. Surmounted by banks of serving machinery above the spine and buttressed by the main roof masts, the building has a strong vertical emphasis.

Logical, efficient, flexible and durable, and in its expressive use of services as sculpture, INMOS has something of the poetic quality of Pompidou and Lloyd's.

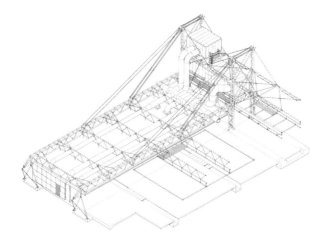

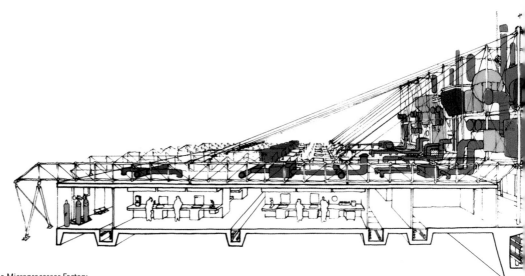

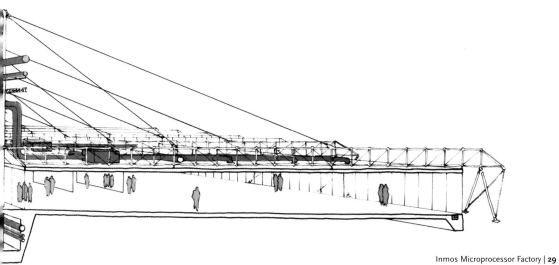

The European Court of Human Rights

The Strasbourg court is a key building in the history of RRP and one of the few landmarks which provide a credible architectural image for the new Europe. The site is away from the historic centre of the city but close to the river. RRP aimed to create a symbolic landmark but not a monument: the nature of the Court's business implies that its premises should be anything but intimidating or fortress-like. Rather it should be welcoming and humane, while preserving an appropriate dignity. Protecting and enhancing the quality of the site was another prime objective, while economy of running and a 'natural' environment were almost equally important.

The basic diagram of the scheme was tested to the limits during the design process – the collapse of the communist bloc greatly increased the European 'family': the building's office provision had to grow by some 50 percent and the public spaces by 25 percent.

The two main departments of the European court, the Court itself and the Commission, occupy two circular chambers, clad in stainless steel, at the head of the building. The entrance hall is a classic RRP interior, light-filled and with fine views out over the river. The 'tail' of the building, divided into two parts, contains offices and administration and the judge's chambers. Functions are clearly legible. Only the main public spaces, focusing on a stone-paved rotunda, are air-conditioned (using an economical heat-exchange system). The remainder of the building relies on natural ventilation (and light) and opening windows – marking a new era in the practice's work. Facades provide for a high degree of planting: greenery is now well established and spills down from the roofs.

The building is a powerful and highly rational expression of the function it serves but is imbued too with a Mendelsohnian streak of romantic expressionism.

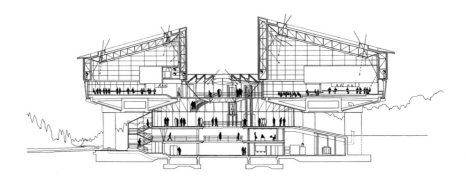

Channel 4 Television Headquarters

The Channel 4 headquarters building occupies a prominent corner plot near Victoria Station, and comprises c.15,000 square metres of headquarters, broadcasting suites and a studio, an underground car park and a landscaped garden square. The building, clad in pewter-coated powder-grey aluminium and glass, occupies the northern and western sides of the site. Residential developers, using their own architects, built the apartment blocks that form the southern and eastern edges of the site.

The two four-storey wings contain office space accommodating up to 600 staff and are arranged in an L-shape, addressing the corner of the street with a curved connecting space framed by two 'satellite towers'. To the left are four conference rooms stacked one on top of the other, and to the right lifts, boiler flues, and chiller plant, topped by transmission antennae. The entrance, through a dramatic concave suspended glazed wall, is the predominant feature of the scheme. A stepped ramp leads from the street over a glass bridge spanning the roof-light of the foyer/cinema complex below. Beyond the reception area a restaurant fills the curve with views over the garden. A sweeping roof-top terrace extends from the top-level board room.

The clients were looking for a scheme which expressed the character of their operations – innovative, socially aware and willing to take risks. The building admirably expresses the perceived identity of the organization while reflecting civic and contextual values which are central to RRP's urban architecture.

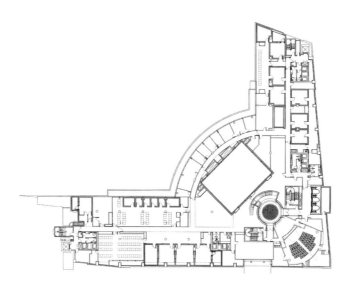

Bordeaux Law Courts

In 1992 Richard Rogers Partnership won the international competition to design new law courts for the historic city of Bordeaux. The team designed a building that would, through its feeling of transparency and openness, create a positive perception of the accessibility of the French judicial system, whilst also incorporating significant sections of the medieval city wall and towers. This is one of the most significant projects by RRP in recent years and marks a distinct phase in the design philosophy of the practice.

While respecting the historic setting and recognising the civic significance of the new building, the practice was anxious to produce a design that was not overly deferential – the intention was to design a simple box, like Beaubourg, that clearly reveals its function and organisation. The brief was complex, requiring complete separation of public and judicial circulation patterns – by pulling the building into its constituent parts, the resulting transparency was intended to encourage a sense of orientation, rendering an historically imposing institution more open and accessible. The result is a powerful conjunction of clear formal concerns that ensures that justice is seen to be done.

Key elements of the design are the creation of public space and integration with the existing urban landscape – the function of the building is legible to all, both from within and without. Public entry to the building is facilitated without pomp, via a flight of stairs placed to the side. The great Salle des Pas Perdus is the core of the building, where lawyers, their clients and the public meet and converse. The seven courtroom 'pods' are clad in cedar wood, raised on pilotis above the limestone plinth within a great glass curtain wall under an undulating copper roof. The administrative offices are reached by bridges spanning the atrium and the clarity of the plan ensures that different routes across the atrium are maintained for both public and magistrates – emphasising function whilst ensuring sufficient levels of security. A new restaurant and restored medieval tower provide a dining space for the judges and magistrates. With its use of irregular forms and natural materials, the building successfully complements its sensitive environs, including a section of the city's medieval wall and the great gothic cathedral opposite.

In the case of Bordeaux, the practice has revisited the issue of services, capitalising on the significant advances in 'green' technology. The emphasis is on effective passive control systems: the 'containers' beneath an undulating roof and the fenestration systems (manually-operated 'brise-soleils' along the western facade). The flask-like volumes of the courtrooms allow daylight deep into the internal spaces and, through their great height, ensure temperature control through stratification. Their form was continually refined through three-dimensional modelling so as to be justifiable on geometric, technical and constructional grounds – that said, there is a certain serendipity (given the geographical area) in their similarity to wine-flasks. By optimising all practical considerations, the design solution for the courtrooms is appropriate aesthetically, socially and iconographically. The great glazed box wrapping around the chambers, with its sun-screening and ventilation systems incorporated within the roof, functions as a 'breathing' container. In addition, the podium and offices are built in heavyweight concrete construction – resulting in an effective passive heat control system.

The High Tech aesthetic of the building places great emphasis on assemblage – how the distinct parts fit together, with particular attention paid to the junctions of elements which have been attenuated and honed. Highly modelled, these junctions take on a sculptural quality with every nut and bolt carefully considered and organised. The intention is an organic completeness established throughout the entire building – perhaps a subconscious reference to the Centre Pompidou, the building which marked the beginnings of the Richard Rogers Partnership.

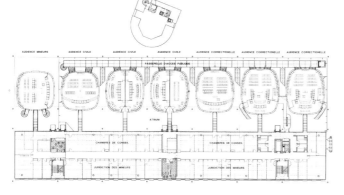

Daimler Chrysler Office and Retail

In 1991 the city authorities opted for a thoroughly conservative masterplan for the redevelopment of the devastated Potsdamer Platz quarter of Berlin (close to the former line of the Berlin Wall), rejecting more radical proposals including those by RRP. A further competition for the Daimler Chrysler site was won by Renzo Piano and Christoph Kohlbecker. RRP was subsequently commissioned to design three buildings on the site with a total area of 57,800 square metres.

The brief stipulated that RRP work within the context of the traditional Berlin square block, with buildings no more than nine storeys high formed around potentially oppressive internal courts. To one side, the buildings had to address an enclosed retail arcade raised several storeys above ground level. Working within these constraints, the practice was able to subtly subvert the municipal masterplan to produce buildings of strikingly contemporary appearance which, most significantly, utilised a low-energy servicing agenda.

The key to this strategy was the erosion of the blocks at their south-east corners to allow daylight to penetrate the central courts, which were turned into covered atria to illuminate interiors, and to facilitate views out of the buildings. The atria are naturally ventilated throughout the year, with heating mechanically augmented in winter. The two office buildings and one residential block were designed for natural ventilation throughout, with intensive research by the RRP team and specialist consultants into the servicing programme partly funded by an European Union grant. As a result, it was estimated that energy consumption in the office buildings would be half that generated by a conventionally air-conditioned building. The facades of the buildings incorporated clear and opaque glass panels, solid areas of ceramic tile cladding, and external and internal blinds, a sophisticated mix which allowed the internal environment to be adjusted in response to the requirements of users. Visually striking, RRP's contribution to the Potsdamer Platz development challenged conventional wisdom, producing a pioneering low-energy environment for business accommodation.

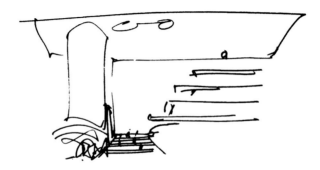

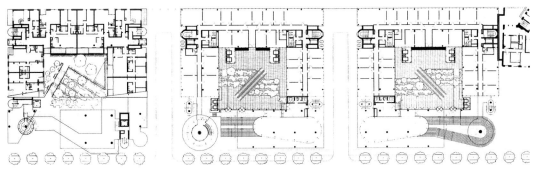

VR Techno Plaza

Rogers' initial role in the development of the VR Techno complex at Gifu was to prepare a masterplan to accommodate ten buildings on the steep hillside site, covering around 16 hectares, retaining where possible the natural contours of the land.

VR Techno is a government-led research centre providing facilities for advanced technology companies with a special interest in virtual reality issues, providing educational, communal and laboratory/office spaces as a resource for private research bodies and the general public.

RRP was commissioned to design two buildings on the site, the Techno Plaza and a subsequent research building for the Amano pharmaceutical company. Techno Plaza is a strong response to the natural landscape, with two distinct elements – offices and research laboratories. The building has an exposed concrete frame with retaining walls and floor slabs partially buried or planted to enhance thermal mass, ensuring maximum benefit from the stable ground temperatures and discouraging rainwater run-off. Glazed facades are equipped with louvres to control solar gain and a stainless steel clad ventilated roof further reduces the energy load on the building. External, planted terraces provide views across the valley.

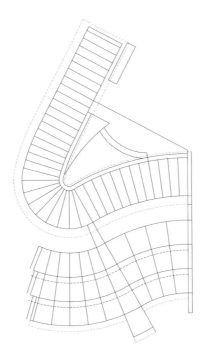

88 Wood Street

The first City building completed by RRP since Lloyd's of London in 1986, 88 Wood Street demonstrates the potential for speculative commercial development that does not compromise on quality and enhances the public domain.

The site, at the junction of Wood Street and London Wall, was formerly occupied by a 1920s telephone exchange. Delays in securing the demolition of this supposedly 'historic' building, combined with the onset of an economic recession in the 1990s, led to the cancellation of a 1990 scheme for a prestige new headquarters for banking corporation Daiwa. A larger scheme was designed in 1993–94, with speculative letting in mind.

The 33,000 square metre building is arranged as three linked blocks of office accommodation that step up from eight storeys on Wood Street, where the context includes two listed buildings, to 14 and finally 18 storeys to the west, responding to the taller built topography towards London Wall. By using the extensive basement of the demolished telephone exchange for plant, roof levels were kept largely free. The office wings are constructed of in-situ concrete which contrasts with the lightweight, steel-framed service towers containing toilets, lifts and dramatic, fully glazed stairs. The use of brilliant colour enhances their impact – air intakes and extracts at street level are also brightly coloured, contrasting with the neutrality of the occupied floors.

The generosity of the scheme is reflected in the spacious, eight metre-high entrance lobby, floored in granite as an extension of the external landscaping. This reception area features a 54 metre-long wall running the length of the building. The facades of the main office floors are glazed from floor to ceiling to maximise daylight and views – in addition, levels 8,12 and 16 lead directly onto roof terraces with spectacular views over the City skyline.

Though built to a strict commercial budget, 88 Wood Street contains many innovative elements. The massing of the building allows controlled daylight to penetrate the office floors. Its triple-glazed active facade is formed of single panels, each three metres by four metres, of highly transparent float glass. The inner faces of the external panes have a low emissivity coating which further reduces internal solar gain, while the cavity between the double glazed units and the third panel is fitted with motorised, integral horizontal blinds with perforated slats. Photocells on the roof monitor external light conditions and adjust the angle of the blinds, thus minimising sun-glare, heat gain and energy consumption.

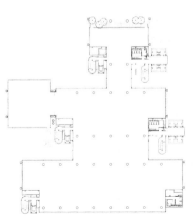

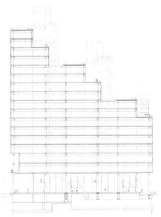

Montevetro

The Montevetro residential development occupies a site at Battersea Reach, south of the Thames and looking across to Chelsea's Cheyne Walk. The site was formerly occupied by an early 20th-century flour mill, closed during the 1980s. Its context is extremely varied – to the east, high-rise 1960s housing, surviving older terraces and villas and, to the west, the listed 18th-century church of St Mary at the river's edge.

By inflecting the new building, RRP aimed to create variety along the river-walk. The major public gain is the riverside park which has created a continuous route between Wandsworth and Battersea bridges, while also enhancing the setting of St Mary's.

The scheme consists of five connected blocks which step down to four storeys where it abuts the church, rising to a full 20 storeys on the north-eastern extremity of the site. Lift and staircase towers connect the blocks, giving Montevetro a strongly modelled profile and providing access to all apartments without resort to internal corridors. The western facade of the development is heavily glazed, providing magnificent views over the river, Chelsea and, from upper floors, much of west London. The 103 apartments which range in size from approximately 95 to 230 square metres are all provided with generous balconies overlooking the river. The east facade, animated by the lift towers, has a more solid aesthetic with panels of terracotta cladding. Health and leisure club facilities are provided in a low-rise block adjacent to the street.

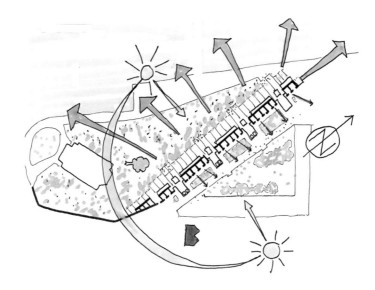

Lloyd's Register

Lloyd's Register (an organisation totally separate from that of Lloyd's of London) is an old-established City institution, its Fenchurch Street headquarters the centre of a worldwide operation. The growth of the business during the 1980s and the planning constraints on developing the congested Fenchurch Street site made Lloyd's Register consider moving out of London. In 1993, RRP was commissioned to prepare proposals for developing a greenbelt site at Liphook in Hampshire. The Liphook scheme, featuring low-rise, naturally ventilated pavilions sunk into a mature landscaped park, marked a significant phase in RRP's developing interest in low-energy, sustainable design. The scheme was, however, abandoned in the face of planning objections and in 1995 Lloyd's Register commissioned RRP to prepare proposals for its City site.

Set within a conservation area, access to the headquarters is through a landscaped churchyard. The site is largely surrounded by existing buildings, including 71 Fenchurch Street constructed for Lloyd's Register in 1901. This Grade II listed building has been incorporated into the new headquarters and extensively restored. The original building retains a general committee room, chairman's office and smoking room, and now includes a conference suite with a 50-seat auditorium. The new building comprises fourteen stories of office space and two basements. The brief called for a net lettable area of 24,000 square metres.

The floorplates of the new building taper in response to the awkward geometry of the site, creating a fan-shaped grid composed of vaults formed around two dramatic atria spaces. This design allows daylight penetration and provides thermal buffers between the offices and the external environment. The building steps up from six levels to 14 levels within the centre of the site.

Service cores are expressed as towers – two primary circulation cores face the churchyard, while secondary cores to the rear house toilets, good lifts and staircases, as well as main services risers. Highly transparent glazing offers instant legibility – people using the fully glazed wall-climber lifts and stairs animate the building's exterior.

The main glazed facade is designed to maximise daylight while limiting solar heat gains in summer and heat losses in winter. In addition to double glazing, the east and west facades feature panels of motorised louvres which control solar energy ingress. Activated by photo-cells mounted at roof level, when the louvres are angled at 45 degrees the facade system reduces solar heat gain by 90 percent.

Working in conjunction with the louvred facades, chilled beams incorporating sprinklers, lighting and a PA system cool the air in the office space. Treated fresh air is supplied through a floor plenum and extracted at high level. The building's energy efficiency means a reduction of carbon-dioxide emissions by 33 percent and of costs by 40 percent when compared with those of a conventionally air-conditioned building.

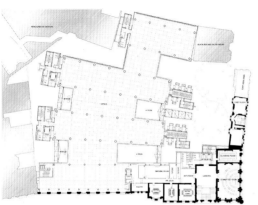

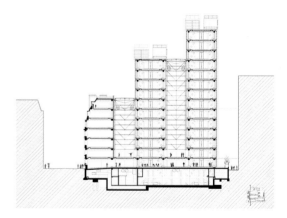

Minamiyamashiro Elementary School

Minamiyamashiro is a remote village in the Kyoto Prefecture nestling in the mountainous region south of Kyoto. Recognising a growing decline in rural population, the local mayor was anxious to reverse this trend by initiating a project that would reunite and regenerate the local community – a school with an extended role as a community centre. After a protracted political battle (originally designed in 1995–96, the building was finally constructed in 2001–03) the result is a building that has restored a sense of identity and civic pride. Prominently located on the main road to the village, the school stands on the brow of a hill, with panoramic views over the countryside beyond.

The brief called for a low-budget school for 6–12 year olds that would also provide community centre facilities for the village – a radical departure from the Japanese norm. The 6,200 square metre building has been conceived as 'a big house', offering not only day-time schooling but evening classes/life-long learning for the community's adult population.

The heart of the school is a large common hall that mediates between the outdoor playing fields and two levels of flexible classroom spaces arranged within a repetitive framed grid of 8.1 by 8.1 metres. This multi level top-lit space is similarly organised within the expressed structural grid and contains all circulation and classroom breakout spaces. Specific spaces for art, science and music classes are grouped at the lower level. A sequence of modular north lights bringing light deep into the heart of the building. An adjacent gymnasium/village hall, built from the same kit of parts, frames the approach to the school and the playing field (including an outdoor swimming pool) which it contains on two sides. Bright wall colours within the grid frame are coded for children and adults, defining different areas and functions.

Detailed and implemented by RRP's Tokyo office, this project uses simple, durable, low maintenance materials to achieve elegant results. The building has a strength of its own, yet can be read within the classic Japanese constructional tradition which has long inspired modern architects.

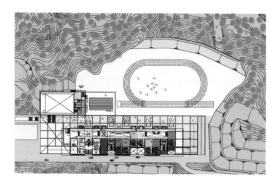

Broadwick House

Bespoke office buildings, like Lloyd's of London or Lloyd's Register, are often mould-breakers. The speculative development sector tends to be more cautious and certainly less likely to challenge planning constraints which reduce the potential for innovative design. In this light, Rogers' Broadwick House comes as something of a surprise. The building was commissioned by a developer and stands in the Soho conservation area, where straightforwardly 'contextual' design has been the norm. The planning negotiations for the project were protracted but the result is a strikingly contemporary structure that enhances the neighbourhood.

The site is an island, with thoroughfares on all four sides. To the east, it abuts Berwick Street, with one of London's best-known street markets. Neighbouring buildings range from Georgian town houses to 1960s high rise flats and crass 1980s Post-Modernist office blocks. Into this diverse scenario, the Rogers scheme introduces an element of calm, rationality and urbanity. By concentrating service cores on the western edge of the block, clear, well-lit and highly transparent office floors are created behind fully glazed facades. Energy efficiency is ensured with the provision of solar performance glazing, in conjunction with external shading devices and motorised blinds. Ground floor facades are set back to facilitate passage along the crowded streets – ground floor and basement areas are allocated for retail and restaurant use, whilst at the fifth floor, the building steps back to provide outdoor terraces. The most distinctive element of the scheme is the double-height space set below the great arched roof, affording spectacular views over London's West End. The glazed lift tower on Broadwick Street is a memorable urban marker, a celebration of movement typical of RRP.

Crisply detailed and using a carefully selected palette of materials, this modest (4,252 square metres), but distinguished addition to the Soho scene has been let to the London design studio of motor giant Ford.

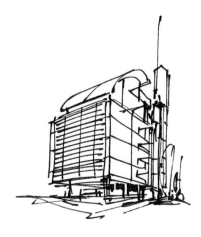

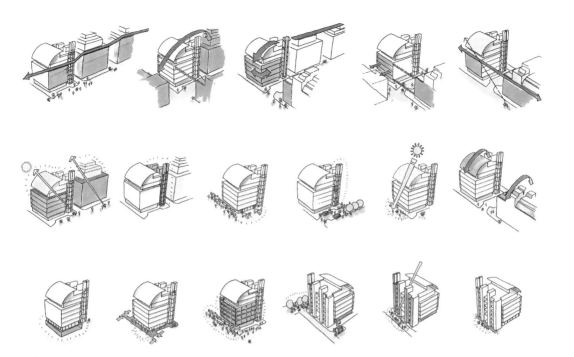

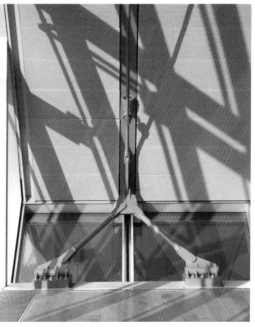

Millennium Experience

Commissioned to mark the beginning of the new millennium, the Millennium Dome was intended as a celebratory, iconic, non-hierarchical structure offering a vast, flexible space. Although a high-profile project in its own right, the building also formed a key element of the masterplan by RRP for the future development of the entire Greenwich Peninsula.

The Dome attracted intense media coverage and generated more political and public debate than any other British building of the last 100 years. For RRP, the project was a resounding success – the building itself was remarkably inexpensive (£43 million for groundworks, perimeter wall, masts, cable net structure and the roof fabric) and the practice devised a non-adversarial procurement route involving standardised components that delivered the building within fifteen months and under budget. Its content, however, was altogether less successful and was savaged by the press.

Mike Davies, project director, and Gary Withers of 'Imagination' together plotted the projection of the comets and stars, dawns and dusks onto the Dome's surface prior to its detailed structural rationalisation. For Davies, an enthusiastic astronomer, the idea of time was uppermost in his mind – the 12 hours, the 12 months, and the 12 constellations of the sky which measure time are all integral to the original concept. Indeed the 12 towers are intended to be perceived as great arms, out-stretched in celebration.

Designed in association with engineers Buro Happold, the key objectives were lightness, economy and speed of construction. The Dome is firmly rooted in the early work of the practice, in particular INMOS, Fleetguard, Nantes, the dome which formed part of the Royal Docks masterplan and the Autosalon at Massy, all of which are assisted span structures.

The structure solved with great elegance the problem of how to enclose and protect the separate exhibition 'zones' from the vagaries of the British climate. Providing 100,000 square metres of enclosed space (2.2 million cubic metres), the structure is 320 metres in diameter, with a circumference of one kilometre and a maximum height of 50 metres. The Dome is suspended from a series of twelve 100 metre steel masts, held in place by more than 70 kilometres of high strength steel cable which in turn support the Teflon-coated glass fibre roof.

The Dome is now being converted into a sports, leisure and entertainment complex, with the potential to become an Olympic venue should London's bid for the 2012 Games be successful.

Chiswick Park

The business parks created in such large numbers during the 1990s – Stockley Park, near London's Heathrow Airport was probably the best of its breed – were generally out-of-town developments dependent on the private car. The worst examples were typified by buildings stranded in large expanses of parking.

Chiswick Park is a business park developed on a different theme. It is located within an existing built-up area on a brownfield industrial site and is largely dependent on public transport – when complete, 75 percent of those working there will arrive either on foot, or by bicycle, bus or train. The spectacular green parkland forming the heart of the site, managed on eco-friendly lines, is public space, open to all and includes an open-air performance area, a lake and nature reserve.

The 33-acre site was formerly a bus works (demolished in the 1980s) and is located off Chiswick High Road in west London, close to Gunnersbury Station and within easy reach of other Underground stations. When complete, the project – which has already won numerous awards – will offer c.140,000 square metres of office space spread between twelve buildings, plus restaurant/bar, swimming pool and fitness centre. Beneath each building provision is made for car-parking and plant. Six four-storey buildings have so far been completed; subsequent phases will include a mix of five, nine and 12 storeys.

In contrast to those at Stockley Park, the buildings at Chiswick are standardised, using off-site construction technology, securing economies of time and cost – to date the six buildings have taken approximately nine months to construct. The project reflects the conviction of developer Stanhope that high quality can be achieved using standardised components and construction management procurement. The aim was to produce a development that is highly distinctive and yet buildable within commercial constraints. The office buildings contain highly flexible space that can be configured in open plan or cellular form.

The clarity of the building plan – a central core surrounded by uninterrupted 18 metre deep office plates – is assisted by the use of external escape stairs which contribute to the scheme's distinctive identity. Central atria give views out into the landscaped park and bring light into the heart of each building.

The energy strategy is designed for economy and environmental responsibility – fixed external aluminium louvres and retractable external fabric blinds activated by light sensors together shade 90 percent of the buildings' surfaces. This significant reduction of solar gain makes possible the use of a displacement ventilation system – Chiswick Park's energy efficiency will result in low running costs in the long term.

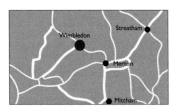

Rogers House
Address: London, United Kingdom
Date of construction: 1968–69
Client: Dr and Mrs Rogers
Project credits: Richard and Su Rogers
Photographers: Richard Bryant, Richard Einzig/Arcaid, Florian Fischotter

Centre Georges Pompidou
Address: Place Georges Pompidou, 75004 Paris, France
Date of construction: 1971–77
Area: 100,000 m²
Client: Ministére des Affaires Culturelles / Ministére de l'Education Nationale
Project credits: Piano and Rogers
Photographers: Richard Bryant, Richard Einzig/Arcaid, Bernard Vincent, RRP Archive, Martin Charles, Paul Wakefield, Yann Arthus-Bertrand/Corbis

Lloyd's of London
Address: 71 Fenchurch Street, EC3M 4BS London, United Kingdom
Date of construction: 1978–86
Area: 55,000 m²
Client : Lloyd's of London
Project credits: Richard Rogers Partnership
Photographers: Katsuhisa Kida, Dennis Gilbert/View, RRP Archive, Grant Smith

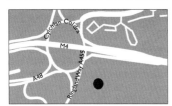

Inmos Microprocessor Factory
Address: Ringland Way, Newport, NP18 2TA Wales, United Kingdom
Date of construction: 1982–87
Area: 8,900 m²
Client: Inmos Ltd
Project credits: Richard Rogers Partnership
Photographers: Ken Kirkwood

The European Court of Human Rights
Address: Council of Europe, 67075 Strasbourg, France
Date of construction: 1989–95
Area: 300,000 m²
Client: Conseil de l'Europe
Project credits: Richard Rogers Partnership
Photographers: Katsuhisa Kida, Morley von Sternberg, Christian Richters, John E. Linden

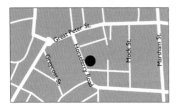

Channel 4 Television Headquarters
Address: 124 Horseferry Road, SW1P 2TX London, United Kingdom
Date of construction: 1990–94
Area: 15,000 m²
Client: Channel Four Television Company
Project credits: Richard Rogers Partnership
Photographers: Richard Bryant/Arcaid

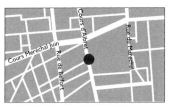

Bordeaux Law Courts
Address: Intersection des Frères Bonies / Cours d'Albret, 33080 Bordeaux, France
Date of construction: 1992–98
Area: 25,000 m²
Client: Ministère de la Justice & Tribunal de Grande Instance
Project credits: Richard Rogers Partnership
Photographers: Christian Richters, Vincent Monthiers, RRP: Amo Kalsi

Daimler Chrysler Offices, Retail & Residential
Address: Linkstraße 4–8, 10785 Berlin, Germany
Date of construction: 1993–99
Area: Office Area Buildings B4 & B6: 29,000 m² Housing Area Building B8: 16,300 m² Retail Area Buildings B4, B6 & B8: 12,500m²
Client: Daimler Chrysler
Project credits: Richard Rogers Partnership
Photographers: Katsuhisa Kida, RRP Avtar Lotay, James Morris

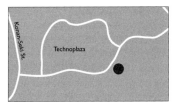

VR Techno Plaza
Address: 4-179-1, Sue-cho, Kakamigahara, Gifu, 590-0108, Japan
Date of construction: 1993–95
Area: Floor Area: 11,462 m², Site Area: 19,945 m²
Client: Gifu Prefecture and VR Techno Centre
Project credits: Richard Rogers Partnership
Photographers: Katsuhisa Kida

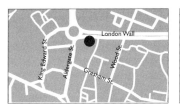

88 Wood Street
Address: London Wall, EC2Y 5EA London, United Kingdom
Date of construction: 1994–99
Area: 33,073 m²
Client: Daiwa Europe Properties
Project credits: Richard Rogers Partnership
Photographers: Katsuhisa Kida, Sector Light, Y. Futagawa+Assoc.

Montevetro
Address: 112 Battersea Church Road, SW11 3NA London, United Kingdom
Date of construction: 1994–2000
Area: 25,000 m²
Client: Taylor Woodrow Capital Developments
Project credits: Richard Rogers Partnership
Photographers: Katsuhisa Kida, Grant Smith, James Morris/Axiom

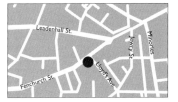

Lloyd's Register
Address: Lime Street, EC3H 7HA London, United Kingdom
Date of construction: 1995–2000
Area: 34,000m²
Client: Lloyd's Register
Project credits: Richard Rogers Partnership
Photographers: Richard Bryant/Arcaid, Peter Cook

Minamiyamashiro Elementary School
Address: 12-26 Nakatani, Minamiyamashiro-mura, Souraku-gun, Kyoto, 619-1411, Japan
Date of construction: 1995–2003
Area: 24,384 m²
Client: Minami-Yamashiro Village
Project credits: Richard Rogers Partnership
Photographers: Katsuhisa Kida, RRP Archive

Broadwick House
Address : 15-17 Broadwick Street, W1 London, United Kingdom
Date of construction: 1996–2002
Area: 32,000m²
Client: Derwent Valley Holdings plc
Project credits: Richard Rogers Partnership
Photographers: Richard Bryant/Arcaid

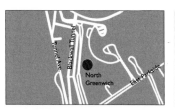

Millennium Experience
Address : Drawdock Road, Greenwich, SE10 OBB London, United Kingdom
Date of construction: 1996–99
Area: 100,000 m²
Client: The New Millennium Experience Company
Project credits: Richard Rogers Partnership
Photographers: Grant Smith, Katsuhisa Kida, Christian Richters, RRP Archive

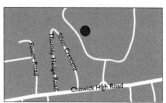

Chiswick Park
Address: 566 Chiswick High Street, W4 5YA London, United Kingdom
Date of construction: 1999–2004
Area: 150,000 m²
Client: Stanhope plc
Project credits: Richard Rogers Partnership
Photographers: Jean de Calan, Grant Smith